Con

GW01460205

This book belongs to

Say the Sounds

y as in funny

s

a

t

i

p

c

k

e

h

r

n

d

g

o

u

l

m

b

ai

j

oa

ie

f

or

w

ng

v

oo

ee

z

th

th

ch

y

x

sh

qu

oo

ue

ou

ar

oi

er

are

you

your

come

some

all

here

they

there

said

Tricky Words

Meet the Characters

Bee

Rags

Inky

Farmer Green

Zack

Ben

Jess

Snake

Hetty

Tolly

Neb

Phonic

Doctor West

Molly

Phonic

This is Phonic.

It was a sunny morning.
Bee, Snake and Inky had gone
to the park.

In a corner of Inky's house was Phonic. It was dark in the corner.

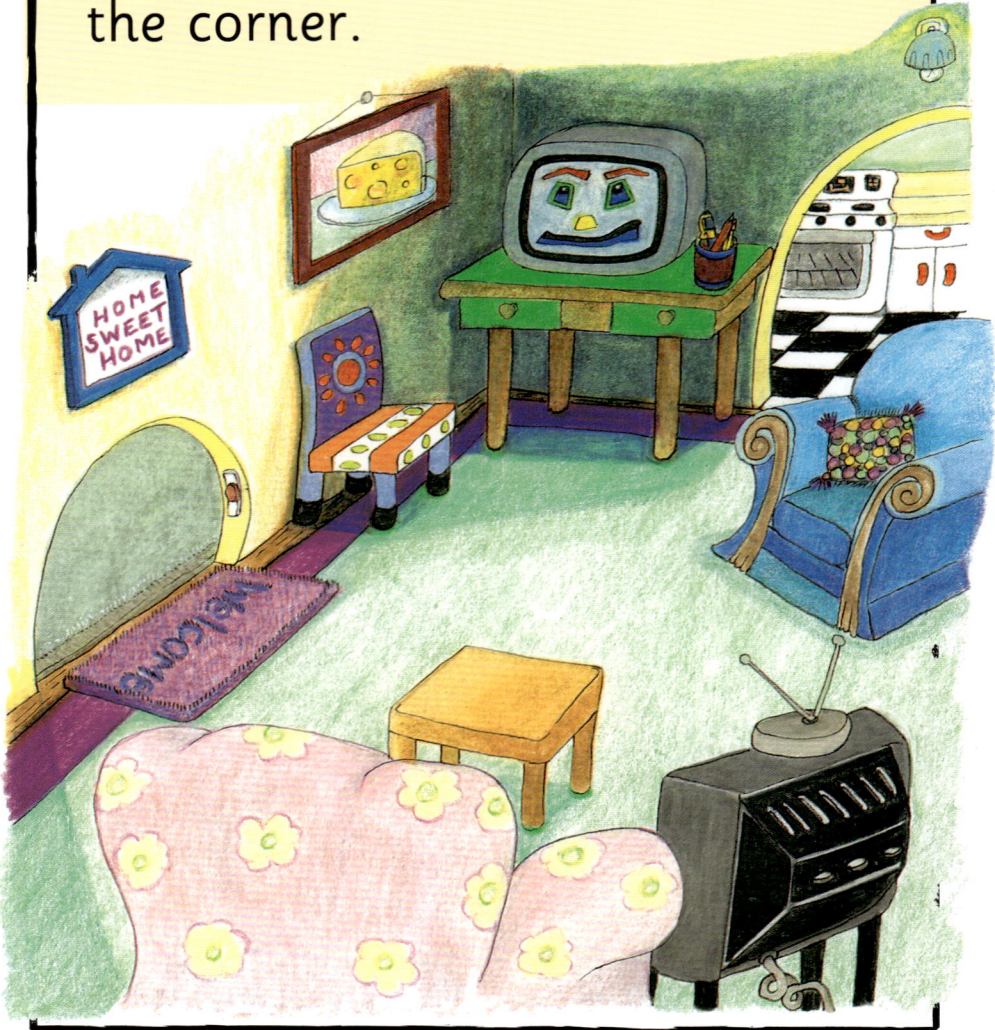

Inky, Snake and Bee ran in.
Inky went to get some drinks.

Yes!

"Did you see that juggler in the park?" said Snake.

"Yes," said Bee.

"He was fantastic!" exclaimed Inky.

"We did have a splendid morning," said Bee.

"Yes," agreed Snake and Inky.

"Well, I am glad *you* had fun," said Phonic. "I see you did not worry about me. I have been stuck here on this desk," he complained.

"We are sorry, Phonic!" cried Bee. "But you cannot come out with us. You need to be plugged in."

"Yes," agreed Phonic, looking sad.

"Hmmmm... I think I have a plan," muttered Inky, and scampered off.

Soon she was back with a big, flat, black box.

"This is a laptop," she said to Phonic. "Load yourself onto a disk."

Then she loaded Phonic's disk onto the laptop, and...

...there was Phonic, up on the screen!

Thank you!

"Phonic can come with us on our next outing," said Inky. "Brilliant!" cried Snake and Bee.

What's in the book?

What is Phonic?
Where had Inky, Snake and Bee
been that day?
Why could Phonic not go
outside with them?

What do you think?

Why is Phonic upset?
How does Inky make Phonic feel better?

Hetty

There are lots of hens on Moat Farm. Every morning, Farmer Green feeds them with corn.

This is Hetty.
She is sitting on her nest.

From her nest she can see the sacks of corn in the barn.

She crosses to the barn and looks around. Ben and Neb are asleep in the sun.

Hetty starts to peck at some corn that has spilled out of a sack.

Molly the cat and her kitten, Tolly, are looking around the barnyard.

28

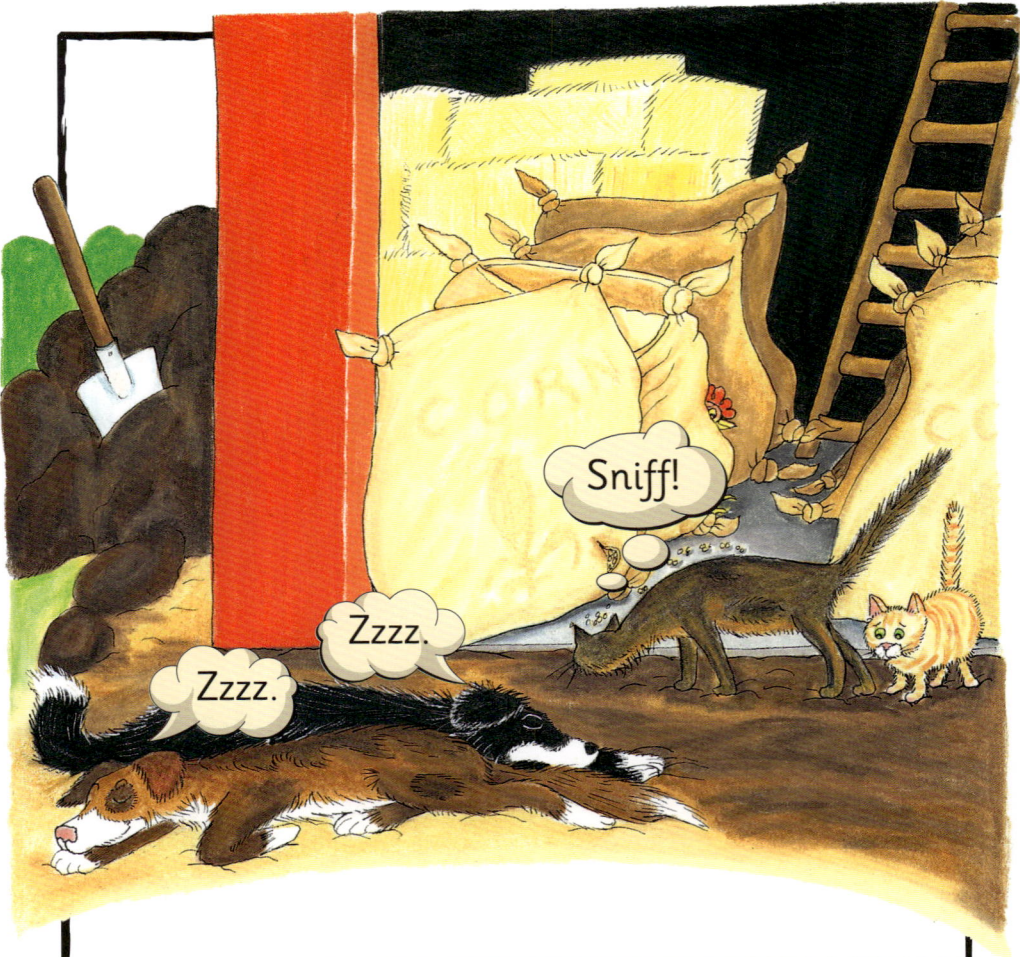

They stop at the barn and sniff.
They can smell something
interesting.

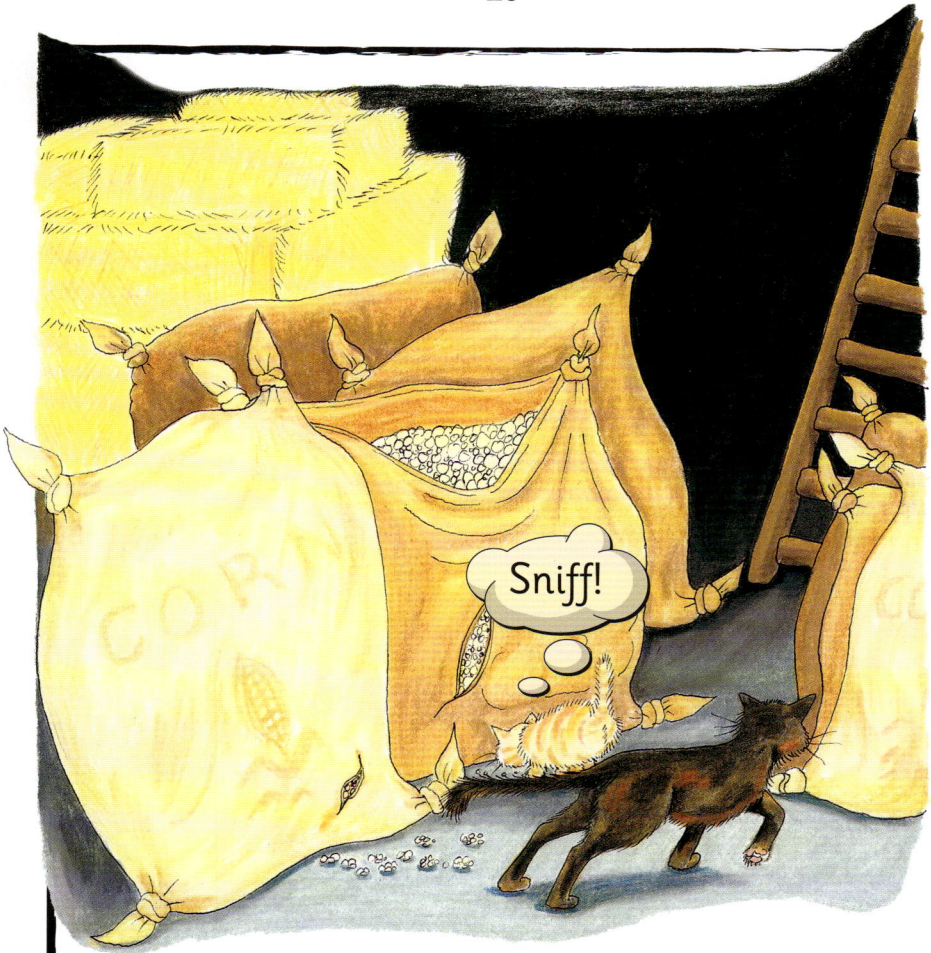

They pad into the barn and creep along. Tolly stops and sniffs at the sack of corn.

Then he pats the sack. In the sack, Hetty feels afraid. She sits as still as she can.

Just then, there is a scratching sound. Molly and Tolly look round, and see rats!

They dash to the corner of the barn and the rats run off.

Lucky Hetty slips quickly back to the hen house and her nest and eggs.

What's in the book?

What kind of
animal is Hetty?
What can Hetty see from her nest?
What do Molly and Tolly
see in the barn?

What do you think?

Why does Hetty hide in the sack?
How does Hetty feel when she
is back on her nest?

Zack's Present

Zack had been given a present.
He was very proud of it.

He sat in the dark. He switched it on and off, on and off, on and off.

He went out and lit things up with it: a slug, a snail and some ants.

Then he went back to his room. "Come and look at this!" he shouted to Jess.

Look at that!

He lit up a cobweb. There was a cobweb pattern on the wall.

"Cool!" said Jess.

"Wait till you see this!" exclaimed Zack.

He pointed under the bed.
Something went scuttling back
into the gloom.

"Yuck! Disgusting!" said Jess and stood up. Zack was still looking under the bed.

"If it is dark, the thing will come back," muttered Zack. He clicked the switch off and waited.

Click!

Just then, there was a snorting sound next to him, and something wet brushed his cheek.

"Help!" he shouted.
"A monster!"

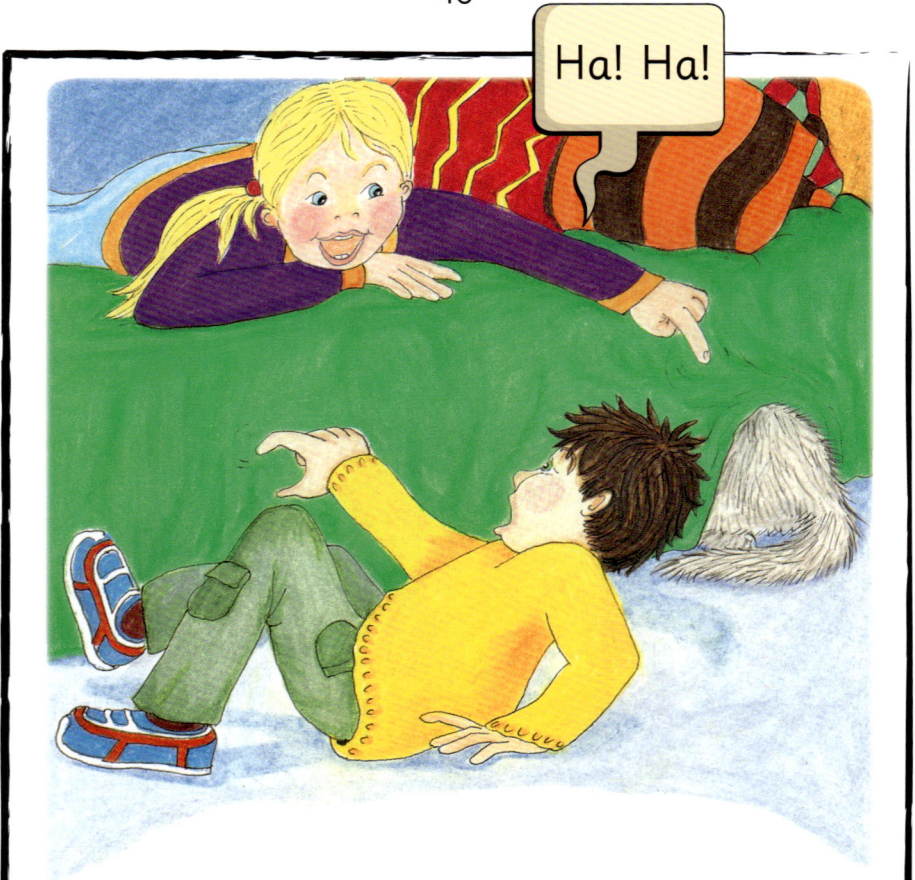

Zack shot out from under the bed. Jess was giggling. She pointed to a tail sticking out from under the bed.

Rags had come to look under the bed too.

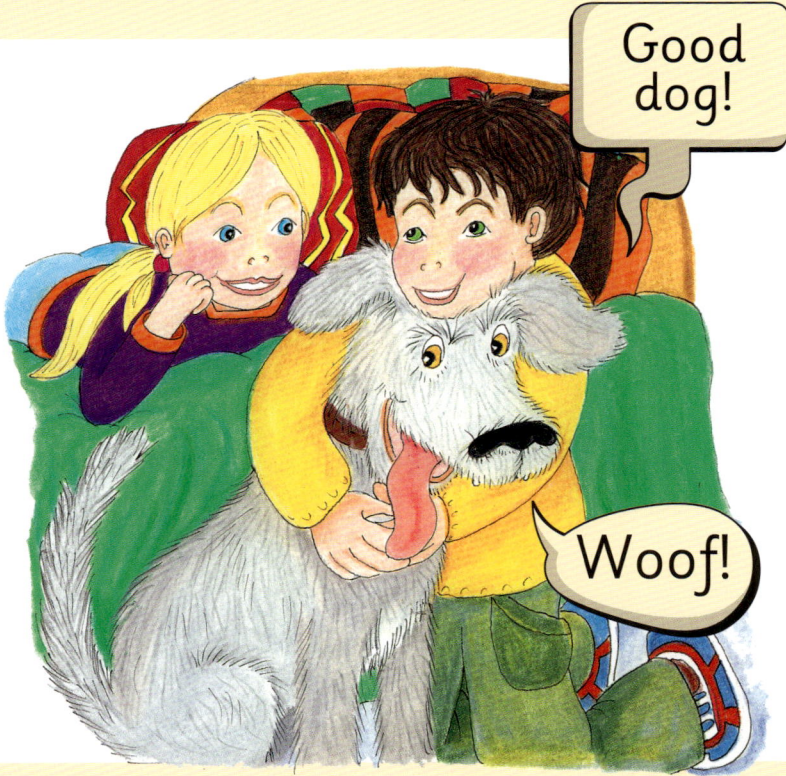

"Thank goodness it was you, Rags, and not a monster!" said Zack.

What's in the book?

What is Zack's present?
What does Zack see outside?
What is under the bed?

What do you think?

Is Zack pleased with his present?
Why does Zack think there is a monster under the bed?

Picnic

It is sunny and Bee, Snake and
Inky have had a picnic.

Snake is asleep and snoring. He has had lots of egg sandwiches.

Bee and Inky are in the forest. They are looking for interesting things.

Under the ground is a big ants' nest. The ants are all rushing about.

They can smell something sweet and sticky. Jam!

Sniff!

Sniff!

They come up to the top of the ant hill and look around.

They see Snake asleep in the sun. They see the picnic things. They see the jam.

The ants collect the jam jar and march back to the ant hill with it.

Bee and Inky come back from the forest. They have found lots of interesting things.

Snake sits up and looks at the things they have found: sweet chestnuts, some twigs and a bit of bark.

You found lots of things!

It will be dark soon.

Snake, Bee and Inky start to pack up the picnic things.

Yuk!

They look and look but they cannot see the jar of jam.

Under the ground, in the ants' nest, the ants are happy.

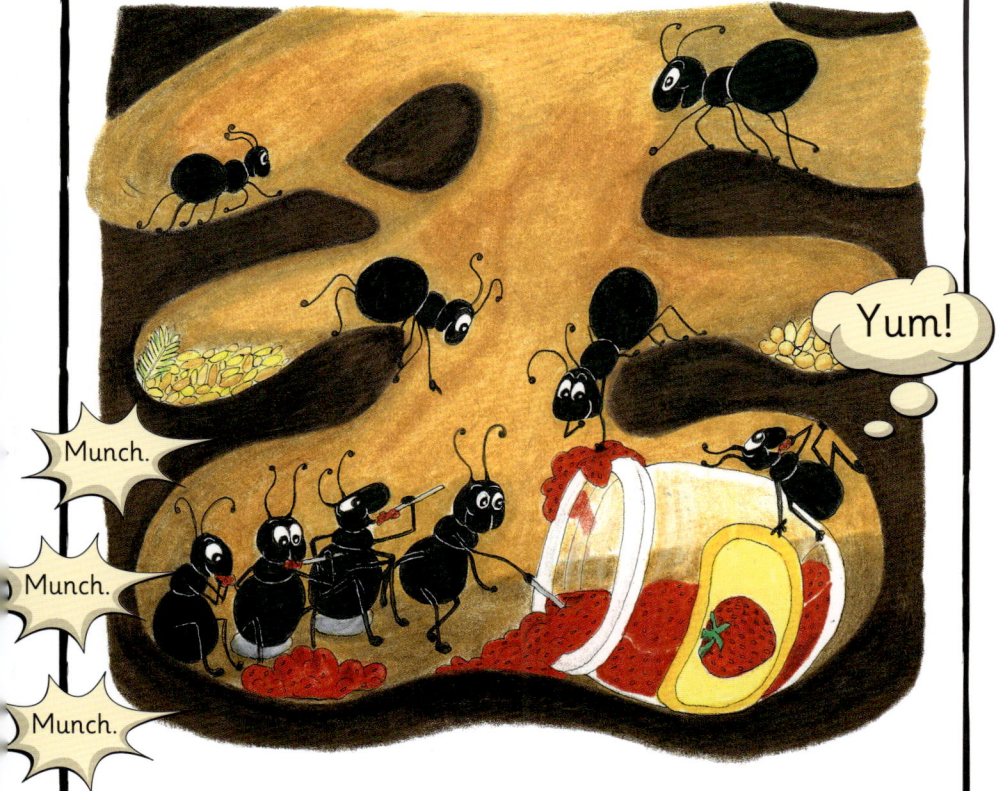

They have lots of jam for dinner!

What's in the book?

What are Bee
and Inky looking for in the forest?
How do the ants know there is
jam in the forest?
Where do the ants take the jam jar?

What do you think?

What is a picnic?
How do the friends feel when they
can't find the jam jar?

Spots

Bee is telling Phonic about Inky. Inky is not feeling well and Bee has sent her to bed.

Bee peeps into the bedroom and sees Inky asleep. She looks again. Inky has big red spots.

Ding dong! Here is Snake. He has come to visit Inky.

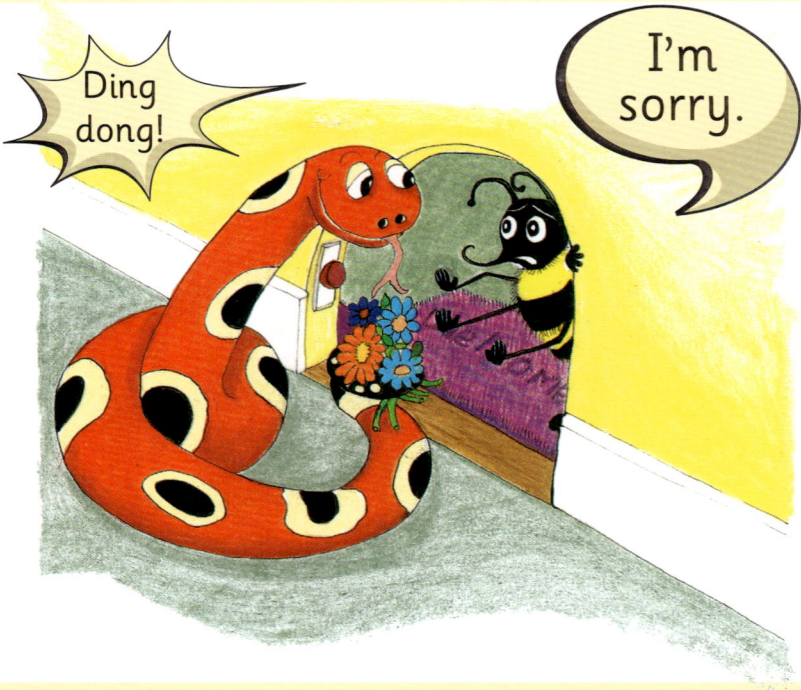

Bee looks at Snake and then at Snake's spots, and will not let him in.

"You have given Inky your spots!" Bee tells Snake. "She is not feeling well at all."

"Er, Bee," interrupts Phonic, "I think you had better look in the mirror."

"I have got spots too!" Bee cries.

Snake and Phonic send Bee to bed as well. Then Snake brings hot drinks for Inky and Bee.

Have a hot drink.

Next morning, Doctor West
visits the house to see Inky and
Bee.

Snake tells Doctor West about the spots, and that Bee thinks she and Inky got them from him.

Doctor West looks at Inky and Bee, and then at Snake. They *all* have spots.

You too, Snake!

Snake has spots on his spots!
  "I am glad *I* cannot get spots,"
thinks Phonic.

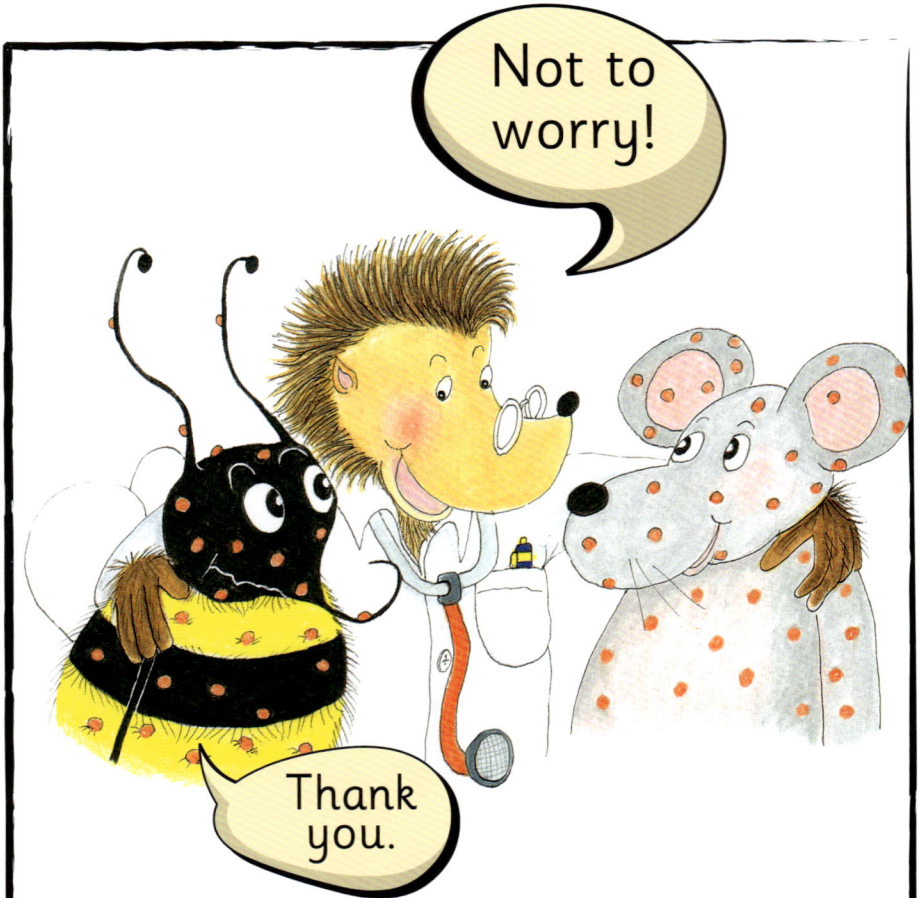

Doctor West tells Bee and Inky that they did not get the spots from Snake, and that they will soon be better.

Inky's and Bee's spots will all vanish, but Snake will have some spots forever.

What's in the book?

Why has Bee
sent Inky to bed?
How does Snake look after
Bee and Inky?
Is it Snake that gives the spots to
Bee and Inky?

What do you think?

Why won't Bee let Snake in the house?
Why will Snake's spots
not all disappear?

Looking for Snake

Bee counts to ten:

"1, 2, 3, 4, 5, 6, 7, 8, 9, 10."

Then she starts to look for
Snake. Snake has hidden.

Is he in the sandbox? Bee looks under the bucket...

Not here!

Not there.

Is he up the tree? Bee flies up and looks at the tree top...

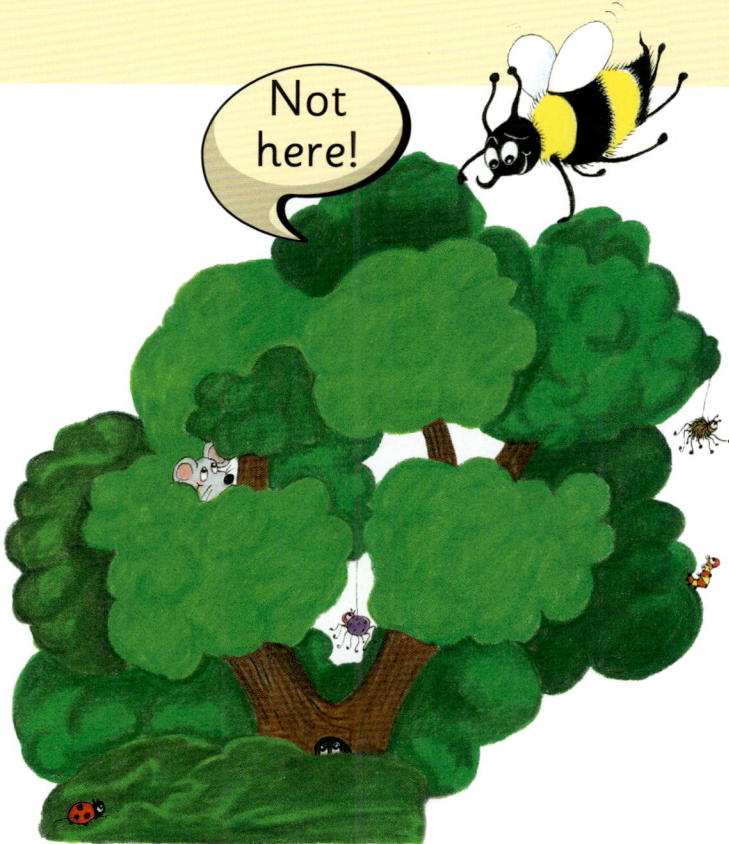

Not here!

Not there.

Is he on top of the shed? Bee looks on the roof...

Not there.

Is he under the shed? Bee looks in the darkness under the shed...

Not here!

Not there.

Bee lands on the ground and looks around.

Snake has hidden in a pot. He peeks out to look for Bee.

Bee is still looking around.
Snake pops back and keeps still.

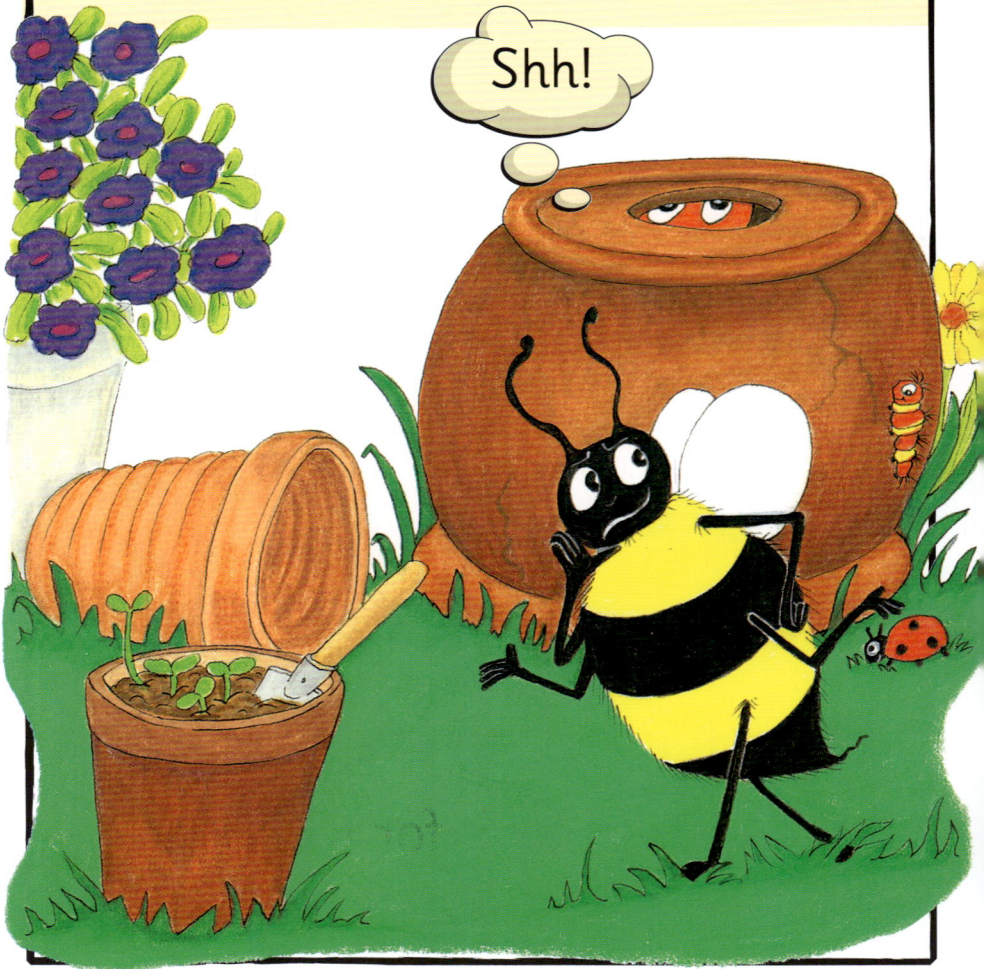

Bee looks.

"Was that a flash of red?" she thinks.

A-ha!

Shh!

Snake keeps as still as he can in the pot.

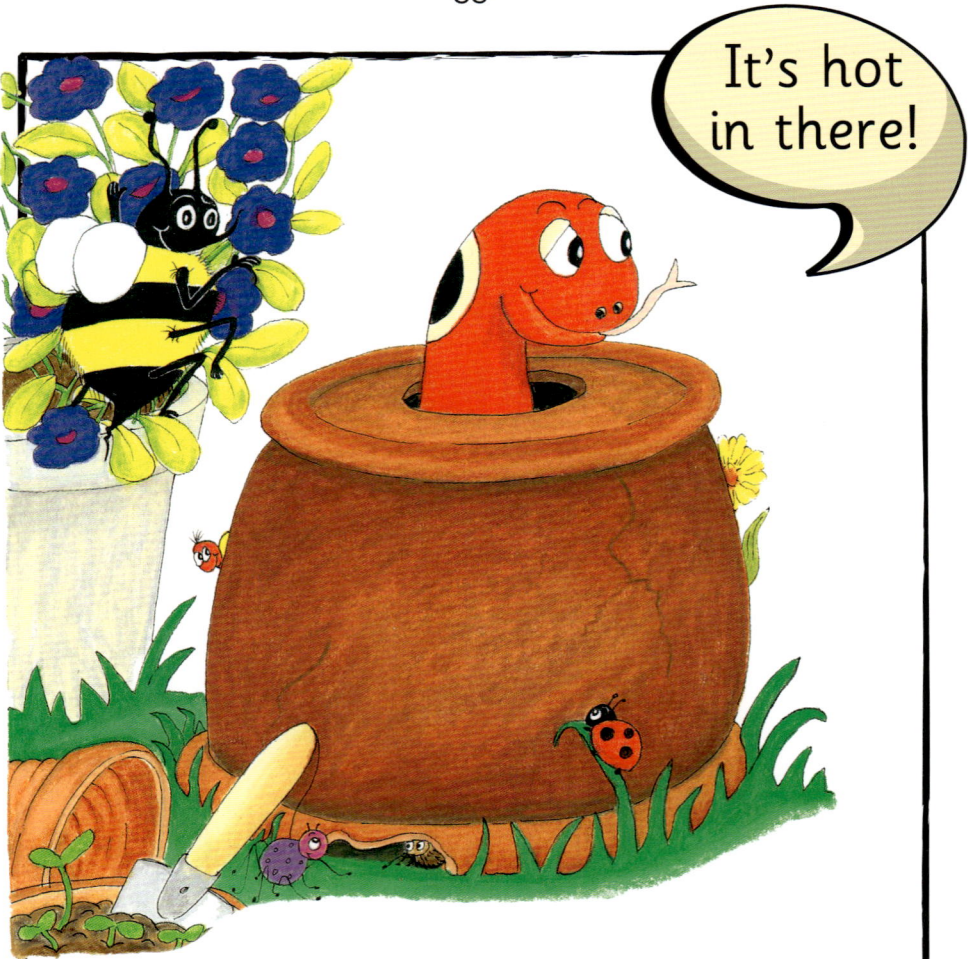

It's hot in there!

Then he peeps up from the pot again.

"There you are!" cries Bee, pointing to Snake. "Found you!"

What's in the book?

What game are
Bee and Snake playing?
Why does Bee fly to the
top of the tree?
Where has Snake hidden?

What do you think?

Why does Snake try to keep very still?
How does Bee find Snake?

Parents

An important part of becoming a confident, fluent reader is a child's ability to understand what they are reading. Below are some suggestions on how to develop a child's reading comprehension.

Make reading this book a shared experience between you and the child. Try to avoid leaving it until the whole book is read before talking about it. Occasionally stop at various intervals throughout the book.

Ask questions about the characters, the setting, the action and the meaning.

Encourage the child to think about what might happen next. It does not matter if the answer is right or wrong, so long as the suggestion makes sense and demonstrates understanding.

Ask the child to describe what is happening in the illustrations.

Relate what is happening in the book to any real-life experiences the child may have.

Pick out any vocabulary that may be new to the child and ask what they think it means. If they don't know, explain it and relate it to what is happening in the book.

Encourage the child to summarise, in their own words, what they have read.

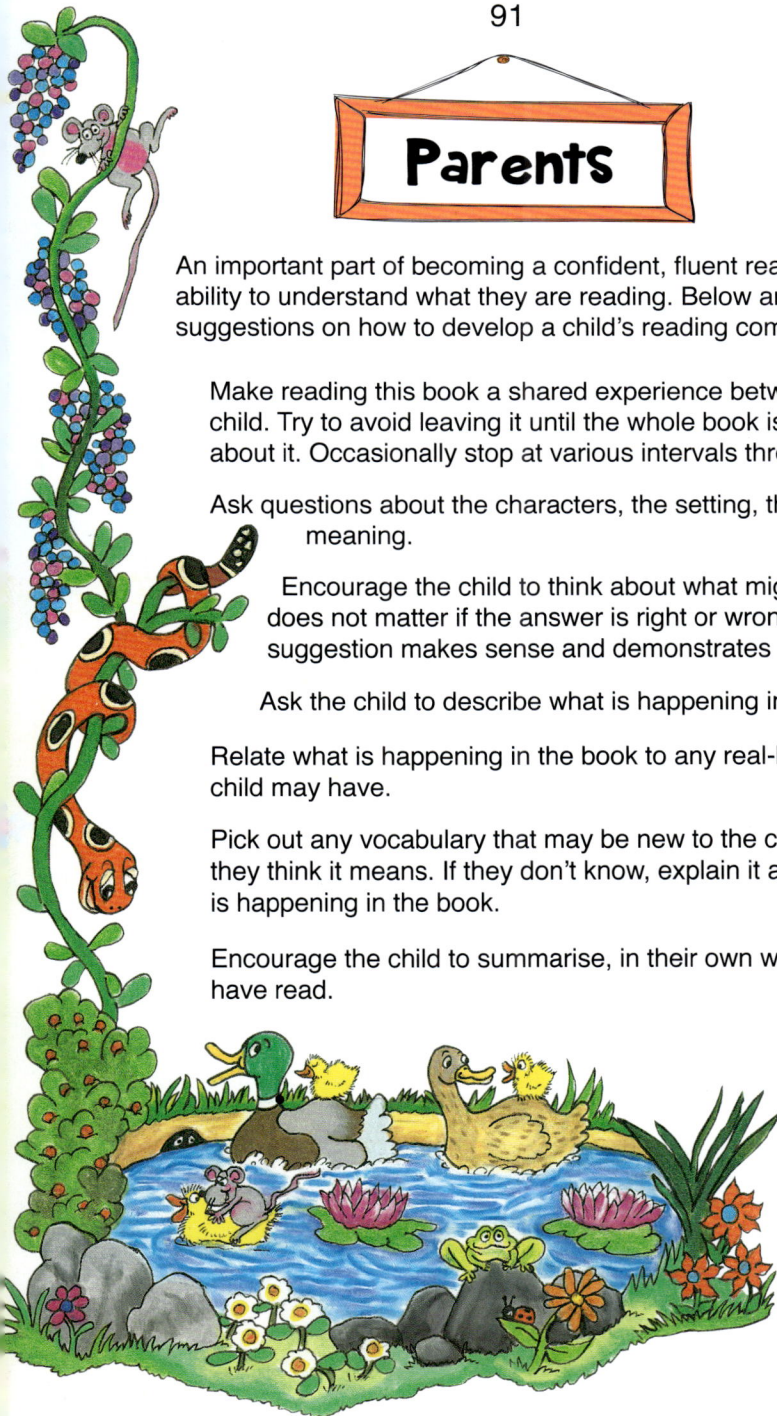

Book Review

Try to answer these questions about each story in this book:

What was the story about?

What happened at the end of the story? Did you guess what was going to happen?

What was your favourite part of the story? Why did you like it?

Which character did you like the best? Can you describe them?

Did you like the illustrations? Why?

Did any parts of the story make you laugh?

Do you think anyone you know would enjoy this book?

Could you re-tell the story in your own words?

Has anything similar to this story ever happened to you?

Would you have liked this story to be shorter or longer?

Were there any parts of the story that you didn't like?

Have you read any stories that are similar to this one?

Would you enjoy reading this story again and would you recommend it to a friend?

Character Review

Choose a character in this book to think about:

What is their name?

Do you know where they live?

Describe what they look like.

What do they do in the story?

Are they good or bad? Why?

Do you like them? Why?

What other things would you like to know about them?